The FIRST BOOK of
ANCIENT ROME

BY
Charles Alexander Robinson, Jr.

PICTURES BY JOHN MACKEY

FRANKLIN WATTS, INC.
575 Lexington Avenue, New York 22

For my grandchildren

FOURTH PRINTING

Library of Congress Catalog Card Number: 59–10952

COPYRIGHT © 1959 BY FRANKLIN WATTS, INC.
Manufactured in the United States of America
by H. Wolff Book Manufacturing Company, Inc.

CONTENTS

ROME

From the beginning of history Italy has been a great center of civilization. In fact, the civilization it developed in ancient days has become the basis of our own.

Rome, the chief city of Italy, created the largest empire the ancient world ever saw. The whole civilized world became a part of the Roman Empire. That meant that everyone from Britain to Persia (now called Iran) was protected by the same armies, was tried by the same law, and paid his taxes into the same treasury. Eventually this world adopted a new, common religion, that of Christianity.

When the Roman Empire finally fell, great modern nations such as England, France, and Italy itself grew from its fragments. When we look around at our modern world and see it divided into many nations, often suspicious of each other and even at war, Rome's achievement seems even more remarkable.

Two things in particular stand out about the Roman of those ancient times. The first was his character. The Roman was a man of his word. He may not have had much pity in his heart, but he was brave and energetic. He respected his forefathers and the gods of the state. Above all, he believed that the laws and ancestral customs must be obeyed.

Another important quality of the Roman was his ability

9

to compromise—to reach an agreement by giving a little in order to take a little. We must never forget that we are dealing with the greatest empire builders in history. Why did Rome succeed where those other empire builders, Greece and Persia and Egypt, failed? The answer must be found in the Romans themselves. Surely character and a devotion to the state and its laws must be given first place, but the ability to compromise is a very rare quality too. The Greeks never had it, and ended their history fighting among themselves.

Roman galley, propelled by oars and a sail

THE FOUNDING OF ROME

Italy begins just south of the Swiss Alps and soon becomes a peninsula running to the southeast between the Adriatic and the Mediterranean Seas. The peninsula is about 650 miles long and is nowhere more than 125 miles wide. The Apennine Mountains run down the whole length of the peninsula like a spine and at places rise to a height of 9,500 feet.

In spite of a shore line of more than 2,000 miles, Italy has only two good harbors: at Genoa and Naples on the Mediterranean coast. The biggest river is the Po in the north, but the most famous is the Tiber, where Rome is located. Rome was not built where the Tiber empties into the Mediterranean, because pirates might suddenly attack such a spot. It was built fifteen miles up the river. Ancient boats could navigate that far, and moreover, at just that point there was an island which made it easier for people to cross the river.

Rome's location in central Italy, near the sea and controlling the ford of the Tiber, meant that trade rapidly became important. Then, too, there was some level ground beside the river, where people could meet and exchange goods. In time the Romans turned this into their market place or Forum, with law courts, temples to the gods, and shops. Round about were the famous Seven Hills of Rome. The most important of these, by far, were the Capitoline, where the city's original

fort was located, and the Palatine, where powerful emperors built their palaces later on.

Every section of Italy had its special name. Rome was situated in the section called Latium, and so the people were called Latins and their language Latin. But the people were similar to the rest of the Italians on the peninsula, and their language was very much the same.

According to legend, Rome was founded in 753 B.C., but archaeologists tell us that its history goes back 2000 years earlier. According to legend, Aeneas, the son of Venus, goddess of love and beauty, grew up in the city of Troy beside the Dardanelles. In 1184 B.C. the Greeks took Troy after a war that had lasted ten years. But Aeneas escaped and after many adventures reached Italy. His son, Ascanius, founded Alba Longa in the Alban Hills across the Plain of Latium from Rome. A descendant, Rhea, had twin sons by Mars, the god of war.

These boys, Romulus and Remus, were set adrift on the Tiber and cast ashore near the Palatine Hill. There they were nursed by a she-wolf, and eventually one of them, Romulus, founded Rome.

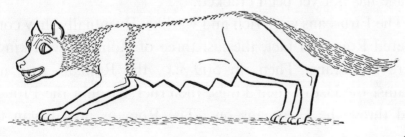

THE ROMAN REPUBLIC

There were two foreign, or non-Italian, peoples in Italy in addition to the Romans and other Italians. One of these were Greeks, colonists sent out by the old city-states of Greece. So many Greeks settled in southern Italy that it became known as Great Greece. The closest the Greeks got to Rome was the Bay of Naples, too far off for warfare between the two peoples, but close enough for the Greeks to trade with the Romans and to give them civilizing influences, such as the alphabet.

The other non-Italians were the Etruscans, who had probably come from Asia. They settled in central Italy in a section later known as Etruria. Today it is called Tuscany, and its chief city is Florence. The Etruscans picked up a good deal of Greek civilization by trading with the Greeks after they arrived in Italy. The vivid paintings in their underground tombs have writing in the Greek alphabet, but no one knows what the writing says because the secret of the Etruscan language has not yet been cracked.

The Etruscans were rich and warlike. Eventually they conquered Rome. In fact, the last three of Rome's seven kings were Etruscans. Then, in 509 B.C. the Romans rose up against the last of their kings, the cruel Tarquin the Proud, and threw the Etruscans out. The Romans now began to

14

Etruscan warriors

create their own form of self-government, or democracy, as we would call it.

It took almost 200 years for the Romans to create a fairly democratic form of government. One reason it took so long was because the nobles—called patricians—tried to keep all the offices for themselves. Eventually the common people—known as plebians—gained privileges.

In place of the king two consuls, or magistrates, were elected each year. These consuls not only had equal power, but could veto each other's acts. In this way the Romans made sure that no man would become too powerful.

At the end of their year in office the consuls had to account to the Senate for what they had or had not accomplished. The Senate was the advisory body of the state and consisted of 300 persons who had originally been elected to office by the common people in their own Assembly.

If a man was ambitious and hoped to become a consul he had first to be elected to lower offices. In these offices he received training as paymaster of the army, as chief of the fire and police departments, and as supervisor of the games and other spectacles. Next he received experience in the administration of justice.

At last he was ready to stand for election as consul. After that he became a proconsul, or governor of a district which Rome had conquered and turned into a province. Then for the rest of his life he would be a member of the Senate. No other state in history has hit upon such a scheme for training men for top government posts. A great deal of Rome's success in conquering the ancient world was due to the great reservoir of able and experienced men she had to draw upon for responsible jobs.

A second reason it took the Romans so long to set up their new government was that they were engaged in constant warfare. Because of their central location in Italy, the Romans had the advantage of being able to march now north, now south against enemies who were always divided. Once they conquered a people, the Romans were tolerant of local customs and were remarkably kind and generous in their treatment of their former enemies. When peace was established, trade began to flourish. Many persons felt that an alliance with Rome was good, certainly far superior to any other alliance possible in those days.

The soldiers of Rome's victorious armies were citizens who were paid by the state. They had to buy their own equipment, however, such as a bronze breastplate and leather shield, an iron sword, and a spear or javelin. Rich people, who could afford horses, made up the cavalry.

The typical military unit of the Romans was the legion. It was composed of 3,000 heavy-armed foot soldiers divided into companies, or maniples, of sixty men each. The special advantage of the legion was that it could be managed with great ease. About 1,200 light-armed troops and 300 cavalry were attached to each legion. These were the men who were soon called upon to fight the Roman Republic's greatest war.

HANNIBAL

Across the Mediterranean Sea from Italy, on the coast of
North Africa, lay the rich city of Carthage. This was a Phoeni-
cian—or as the Romans called it, a "Punic"—settlement.
It was founded about 800 B.C. by Tyre and other ancient
Semitic cities of Phoenicia. Carthage built up her own empire
not only in North Africa, but in Spain and Sicily as well.

Trouble between Rome and Carthage first began in Sicily,
where a great many Greeks had also settled. The Romans
were afraid that the Carthaginians were planning to cross
from Sicily to Italy, so they combined with the Greeks and
defeated the Carthaginians. This was in the First Punic War
which lasted from 264 to 241 B.C.

Rome now had possession of Sicily, which became her first
foreign province. From the many Greeks in Sicily the Romans
began to absorb a great deal of Greek civilization. They
greatly admired Greek literature and art, and started to copy
Greek ways. They even adopted the Greek gods. They said
that the chief Roman god, Jupiter, was the same as the Greek
Zeus; that Jupiter's wife, Juno, equalled Zeus' wife, Hera;
that Neptune, the Roman god of the sea, was the same as the
Greek god Poseidon, and so on. Much of this was a good idea,
since Greek civilization was then more advanced than the
Roman. But when imitation is carried too far, it can kill one's

18

own originality. In imitating the Greeks, more and more Romans stopped thinking things through for themselves.

Naturally, the Carthaginians hated the Romans who had conquered them in the First Punic War. Soon they began to plot their revenge, using Spain as their base for an attack on Italy. The Carthaginian leader was a remarkable young man named Hannibal (249–183 B.C.). It is said that when Hannibal was nine years old his father brought him to an altar and made him swear eternal enmity to Rome.

Hannibal was one of the greatest generals of ancient times. His terrible war with Rome, known as the Second Punic War, raged from 218 to 201 B.C. During these years Hannibal and his army lived far from home, in a hostile land, but they never lost a battle except the most important one, the last.

Hannibal crossed the snowy Alps with 40,000 infantry, 9,000 cavalry, and a number of elephants and came down into sunny Italy. Here the Romans waited for him with 700,-000 infantry and 70,000 cavalry. Hannibal wiped out one Roman army after another. In the battle of Cannae about 70,000 Romans were killed. But the Romans held on with dogged persistence, and most of their allies remained loyal. This helps to prove how wisely the Romans had built up their rule in Italy.

Hannibal's greatest mistake was his failure to take Rome. The reason he failed was that he had never learned how to use battering rams and other siege machinery of ancient times. So certain were the Romans that Hannibal would never take their city that a Roman citizen bought the land on which Hannibal was camped and sold it to another Roman at the regular price. The haughty confidence of the Romans enraged Hannibal, but he was forced to abandon his camping site.

In time, a famous Roman named Scipio was able to take a Roman army over to Africa. This meant that Hannibal had to leave Italy to protect his homeland. When he met the Roman general at Zama, it was Scipio who won.

Roman soldiers attacking with a battering ram

TROUBLE IN THE STATE

During the many years of fighting in Italy, thousands of farms were ruined. When peace was established, the small farmer did not have the money to start all over again, so he sold his land to his rich neighbor. This was the beginning of vast estates in Italy, worked by slaves in huge gangs. As for the small farmer who had sold his land, there was nothing for him to do but go to Rome. Rome was already over-crowded, and the newcomers had trouble finding work to do. They were hungry and unhappy. The Romans, even though they had won the war, were badly hurt by it.

Two brothers, the Gracchi by name, now tried to help Rome by getting the displaced farmers back on the farms. But the rich nobles were unwilling to give up their estates, and the Gracchi failed. For the first time in her history, blood was shed in Rome during a discussion of politics. Class hatred mounted.

Rome had many problems. And yet here she was, the glorious victor of Hannibal and the proud mistress of the western Mediterranean. Soon she would turn east and take Greece and then Asia. Egypt would be an easy conquest, and meanwhile Julius Caesar would conquer Gaul.

Why should there be problems in Rome instead of rejoicing? For one thing, the provinces were not well governed.

21

Too many governors tried unjustly to make a fortune in them. For another thing, many of the citizens who had fought in the army against Hannibal owned no property. They were living in the city with little chance or desire to work. Even so, they insisted on games and other entertainments, and on cheap food. Later on, free food was given them by the government! Many of the jobless were willing to sell their votes to self-seeking nobles.

Rome was now a world capital, beautiful to look at and with famous men in it. But the city lived primarily on the taxes raised in the provinces rather than on manufactures and exports.

Masked dwarfs entertaining a Roman audience

DAILY LIFE IN ROME

At the head of the Roman family was the father, a stern individual who at first had absolute authority, even the power of life and death, over his wife and children. Later on, when this power was broken, the family remained an intimate group for a long time. The wife was respected, and together all the members of the family worshiped the gods and studied the stories about Rome's great past.

A young Roman boy first attended an elementary school where he learned reading, writing, and arithmetic. Then he entered a higher school and studied both Greek and Latin literature and memorized some of Rome's more important laws. Girls had much the same training.

If his parents could afford it, a Roman boy was then taught by a tutor. This was probably a Greek slave who had been captured in one of the wars. A smart boy, if he had the money, could finish his education in Athens, which was a sort of university center.

When he came home to Rome the young man practised public speaking. A good speaker had the best chance of getting elected to public office, and every ambitious youth hoped that some time he would be a consul.

When he reached the age of twenty-five or thirty, a Roman was ready for marriage. His marriage was arranged with the

Romans dressed in togas

girl's father, since she was usually too young to be consulted in the matter. Then too, she was under her father's control.

The marriage ceremonies began with a feast and sacrifices in the house of the bride's father. They ended in the evening with a grand procession to the groom's home. Here he carefully lifted his bride over the threshold, for it was considered bad luck for her to touch the sill of her new home with her foot.

Like their parents, the young couple kept in their house a collection of portraits of famous ancestors. Their own children, as they grew up, would look at the portraits day after day, determined to win fame for themselves.

Life in the family was disciplined and happy. Simplicity was the rule, and it is illustrated by the style of clothing which generation after generation of Romans wore. Both men and women wore a tunic, a plain garment, usually of wool, that came down to the knees. If a man was going to a public meeting, he probably threw over this a toga, a loosely-fitting garment that would have a purple stripe on it if its wearer was a noble.

We have learned a good deal about Roman houses from the excavations of Pompeii. Pompeii was located near the Bay of Naples on the slopes of Mt. Vesuvius, which is still an active volcano. In the year 79 A.D. Vesuvius erupted and buried Pompeii and other nearby towns under a mass of ashes and lava. Apparently the ashes came down on Pompeii in two stages. During the first, many people escaped, but

25

some greedy persons returned, when the ashes stopped falling, to get their jewels. Then the second stage began and these people were buried.

We know this because the Italian archaeologists, in excavating the ancient city, find the outlines of men sometimes half way out of windows with money or jewels in their hands. The archaeologists then pour plaster of Paris into the outlines of these bodies. So, when you stroll around Pompeii today, you come across plaster casts of people who once lived there.

Pompeii is an almost unbelievable sight, a vast dead city. The private houses, the temples and public buildings are there. The paved streets with their ruts, the stepping stones, the little shops and restaurants—all these make you feel that you have really arrived in another world. The ancient water pipes are often in good working order, so that the fountains at the crossings of streets and inside the courtyards of houses still play. Moreover, the Italian archaeologists have dug up the roots of the bushes and trees that once grew in Pompeii and have identified them. They have planted exactly the same bushes and trees all over again, just as they grew in those ancient days.

The typical Roman house, in Pompeii and Rome and elsewhere, did not look very exciting from the street. The walls were plain and windowless. The first room you came to was a reception and living room, which got its light from an opening in the roof above. When it rained, the water that

Interior of a Roman home

poured through the opening fell into a basin which had a fountain and statues. The floors of a Roman living room were decorated with small pieces of colored stone and glass, called mosaics. On the walls were painted brightly colored pictures. Nearby were the rooms where the family records and the portraits of famous ancestors were kept. Further on were the dining and sleeping rooms.

Food was prepared in the kitchen by slaves. The stoves burned wood, and the kettles, frying pans, and other utensils were much like ours today. Bread, cheese, and olives were the chief food, though a moderately prosperous family would have fish, lamb, and green vegetables as well.

Because of the warm climate, most of the life of a Roman family centered in the courtyard around which the house was built. This courtyard was open to the sky. It had columns running around it which gave a shaded walk where people could discuss their affairs if they wished. But most often, probably, the family went right out into the courtyard itself and enjoyed the sunshine. Here were a fountain and beautiful flower beds, bushes, and even trees.

A house such as this belonged to a member of the prosperous middle class. Rich, fashionable people owned large estates and fine houses in the country. The poor were crowded into city tenements sixty feet high. The slaves lived in cramped quarters in the rear of their master's house or in the cellar.

Most men of the ancient world made their living by agriculture. As many things as possible were grown locally because there was no refrigeration in those days and transportation was slow. On the other hand, manufactured articles such as jewelry, pottery, glass, and bricks were carried easily over the fine Roman roads, to be sold in cities and provinces.

There was a regular network of roads throughout the Roman world, not only for the convenience of travelers and the movement of armies, but also for the postal service and business. The most famous Roman road was probably the Appian Way, which runs south from Rome. It is well paved with big blocks of lava, and today automobiles speed along a part of it.

In the Mediterranean the Romans had a regular boat service. The sea journey from Rome to Egypt took three weeks and was the most important of all the services. This was because Rome imported much of her wheat from Egypt, and the common people in Rome were ready to riot if the grain supply fell low.

The population of the Roman Empire at its height numbered about 100,000,000 people, a million of whom lived in Rome itself. Here in the capital was the whole apparatus of government. The many officials lived here. The chief temples and other public buildings were located in Rome.

Rome was also the entertainment center of the Empire. The Circus Maximus, for example, was used for horse races. It was the largest of ancient stadiums and seated over 150,-000 persons. The largest of the many Roman theaters was the famous Colosseum, with a seating capacity of 50,000.

Rome also had more than 800 public baths scattered around the city. A Roman bath had hot, warm, and cold pools, but it was much more than a bathing establishment. Actually, it was a social meeting place, with libraries and lecture halls, race courses, gardens, and rooms for wrestling and boxing.

The opportunity to sponge on the rich, the lively entertainments, and the free food the government provided for the poor attracted people from all over the world to Rome. Rome had become the capital of the world.

Wrestling in a public bath

JULIUS CAESAR

The greatest man Rome ever produced was Julius Caesar. He was born in 100 B.C. of a noble family, the Julian, which traced its ancestry back to gods and heroes. His family, however, was poor, and Caesar was ambitious to become the most important man in the state. He was not powerful enough in the beginning, however, to do this alone.

It so happened that there were two other men at Rome with more or less the same ambitions. One was Pompey, a successful general, and the other was Crassus, the richest man on earth. These two men and Caesar decided to come together in a political alliance. Since they were three in number, the famous union came to be known as a Triumvirate. The Triumvirate planned to try to become masters of Rome. Only the future could tell how they would make out with each other.

For a few years the arrangement worked well. Caesar became consul in 59 B.C., and then left his colleagues at Rome while he himself went off to Gaul as proconsul. What he wanted to do was to gain fame by conquering a large and uncivilized part of the world. Since he was very popular with ordinary folk, he felt sure that his army would become devoted to him. And then, with a highly trained, personal army, he might become dictator of Rome.

31

Of course, this might take several years. While he was away people might forget him. To prevent this, he decided to send back to Rome regular reports about himself. These reports were remarkably modest, but they became famous as the *Commentaries on the Gallic War*. Caesar's account of Roman victories in far-off Gaul (France, as we call it today) thrilled the people of Rome, and it is still widely read in European and American schools.

All Gaul, Caesar says at the start of his book, is divided into three parts. He meant southern Gaul, central Gaul, and the northern part which runs along the Rhine to Belgium and Holland and the North Sea. Caesar conquered the whole area rather easily, for he was a military genius.

Caesar commenced his conquests by subduing a Celtic tribe of Switzerland, named Helvetians. But he learned that German tribes, under Ariovistus and other leaders, kept crossing the Rhine into Gaul, so he decided to march across the Rhine himself and strike terror into the hearts of the Germans. He built a great bridge over the Rhine, the foundations of which still exist.

Caesar also found that the Gauls were receiving help and encouragement from the Britons. So he made two trips across the English Channel and conquered several tribes.

Just when Caesar thought that he had conquered all Gaul the whole land rebelled. The leader of the revolt was a chieftain named Vercingetorix. Caesar cornered him in a fortress at Alesia in 52 B.C. and starved him into surrender.

One method of scaling a wall

During Caesar's conquest of Gaul many people were killed and much property was destroyed. But he probably saved Gaul from the same fate at the hands of the Germans, who at the end would have had nothing to offer but their barbarian way of life. Caesar brought peace and unity and an orderly life to Gaul. He brought opportunities for wide trade with Rome and the Mediterranean. The Gauls absorbed Roman civilization so rapidly that eventually they spoke better Latin than the Romans!

One important result of Caesar's conquests was that he now had a large veteran army that was loyal to him. Back in Rome Pompey was extremely jealous of Caesar and tried to undercut him. As for the other member of the Triumvirate, Crassus, he had lost his life seeking military fame in the East. He had gone to Syria and then attacked Parthia, but he knew little about generalship and he failed.

Not knowing what Caesar might do, the Senate backed Pompey against him. Finally the Senate declared Caesar a public enemy. Two of his friends—Mark Antony and Cassius—were officials known as tribunes. They refused to approve the Senate's action, as tribunes had the right to do. Now they feared for their own lives and fled to Caesar. Caesar knew that he must strike first or he might be ruined.

It was January 11, 49 B.C. Caesar and his army were at the Rubicon, a small river in northern Italy which separated his province from Italy proper. For a proconsul to cross the boundaries of his province into Italy with an armed following was treason to the state, under Roman law. Nevertheless Caesar, having talked the matter over with his friends, crossed the Rubicon and swiftly led his army southward. Pompey and many senators fled before Caesar and went to Greece, where several Roman legions had been stationed.

In 48 B.C., at Pharsalus in Greece, Pompey and Caesar fought it out. Pompey had nine legions, twice as many as Caesar, but the veteran troops of the great general won easily. Pompey fled to Egypt, where he was murdered by one of Caesar's friends.

Egypt in those days was a Greek kingdom. Its queen was the famous and beautiful Cleopatra. When Caesar followed Pompey to Egypt, Cleopatra tried to snare him by her charms, but Caesar was anxious to return to Rome. On his march back he defeated a king of Asia Minor and sent the Senate his famous dispatch, *Veni, vidi, vici* ("I came, I saw, I conquered").

On his arrival in Rome Caesar made himself dictator. Having seized unlimited power, he set to work at once to solve Rome's difficulties. His reforms were many and excellent. He greatly improved the government of the provinces and the collection of taxes, and he allowed many citizens of the provinces to become Roman citizens. This meant that more and more people in the far-flung Roman state were able to enjoy the same advantages of citizenship as those who had been born in Italy.

Caesar also founded many colonies outside of Italy. This

relieved overcrowding in Rome. He started the construction of temples and other buildings in Rome, which gave the people worthwhile jobs. In order to improve the intellectual life of Rome he formed a large library of the best works in Greek and Latin. This library was opened to the public.

Another thing Caesar did was to make a new calendar, consisting of three years of 365 days each, with an extra day every fourth year. The Julian calendar, as Caesar's calendar was called, was used by Europe until 1582. Then Pope Gregory XIII decreed the calendar we use now.

These were only a few of Caesar's reforms. He planned to take a census and to write down and classify the Roman laws. Caesar was remarkable for his military genius, the warmth of his personality, and his fairness to enemies. He was a master of prose literature, and a clear and forceful speaker.

Many Roman nobles, however, envied Caesar and wished to rule in his stead. Various senators formed a conspiracy against him. Among them were the "lean and hungry" Cassius (as Shakespeare describes him) and Brutus, both old friends. As Caesar entered the Senate house on the Ides of March (March 15, 44 B.C.), the conspirators stabbed him to death.

The murder of Julius Caesar was a great crime, for it meant that the Roman world had to go through more civil war before it could settle down to the ways of peace.

36

Caesar and Cleopatra

CICERO

Caesar was a traitor to the state when he crossed the Rubicon and began the civil war against Pompey and the Senate. But it was also true that Pompey and the Senate had been acting illegally in his absence. The times were revolutionary. The common people, hoping to win fuller political and economic equality for themselves, rallied around individuals who merely tried to use them for personal power.

Amid all this confusion stood one great Roman, Cicero, a steadfast champion of the Roman Republic and its constitution. Cicero (106–43 B.C.) was the greatest orator of ancient times and one of the most famous men of all time. He received some of his education at Athens, and then he came back to Rome and entered public life.

Cicero held all the important offices at Rome. This gave him the chance to work for law and order. He discovered that a wicked person named Catiline was plotting to overthrow the government. In a series of brilliant speeches he told his fellow Romans of the conspiracy and saved the state.

Today we have fifty-eight of Cicero's speeches, and about nine hundred of his letters to various friends. Cicero had no idea that these letters would be saved and published, and so he opened up his heart and mind freely. The letters give us a vivid picture of Rome in Cicero's day. The personalities

38

and the crises are portrayed at length and so, too, are Cicero's reactions to them. He had his weaknesses, and occasionally he took too long to make up his mind. But when a decision had to be made, Cicero was firmly on the side he believed to be right.

Cicero was also a literary artist of genius. He wrote a number of philosophical works, the most famous of which is the *Republic*. In it he suggests what he thinks is necessary for orderly government. He believed above all that the various officers of a state should work peacefully together with the help of its leading citizen.

For centuries after he died people copied Cicero's literary style. He is still studied carefully, as are other great writers who lived at the same time. One of these others was Catullus (87–54 B.C.), who wrote some fine lyric poetry. Another was Lucretius (99–55 B.C.), who, in a long poem, *On the Nature of Things*, tried to explain evolution through the movement of atoms.

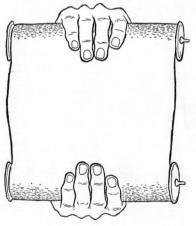

Roman book, written on strips of parchment and rolled into a scroll

39

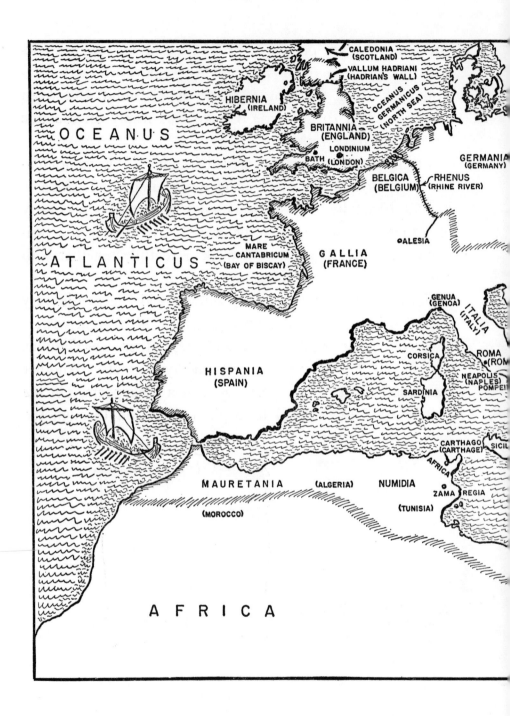

CALEDONIA
(SCOTLAND)

VALLUM HADRIANI
(HADRIAN'S WALL)

OCEANUS
GERMANICUS
(NORTH SEA)

HIBERNIA
(IRELAND)

BRITANNIA
(ENGLAND)

LONDINIUM

BATH (LONDON)

GERMANIA
(GERMANY)

BELGICA
(BELGIUM)

RHENUS
(RHINE RIVER)

OCEANUS

ATLANTICUS

MARE
CANTABRICUM
(BAY OF BISCAY)

ALESIA

GALLIA
(FRANCE)

GENUA
(GENOA)

ITALIA
(ITALY)

HISPANIA
(SPAIN)

CORSICA

SARDINIA

ROMA
(ROM

NEAPOLIS
(NAPLES)
POMPEI

CARTHAGO
(CARTHAGE)

SICIL

AFRICA

MAURETANIA

(ALGERIA)

NUMIDIA

ZAMA REGIA

(MOROCCO)

(TUNISIA)

AFRICA

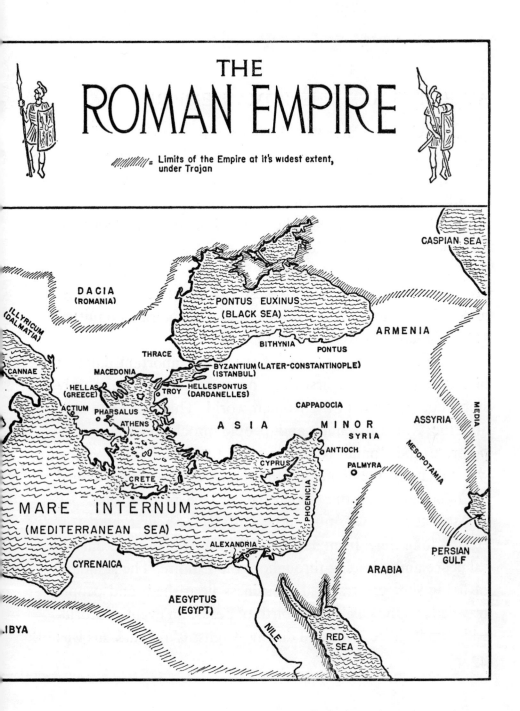

THE
ROMAN EMPIRE

▨▨▨ = Limits of the Empire at it's widest extent, under Trajan

CASPIAN SEA

DACIA
(ROMANIA)

PONTUS EUXINUS
(BLACK SEA)

ILLYRICUM
(DALMATIA)

ARMENIA

BITHYNIA   PONTUS

THRACE

CANNAE

MACEDONIA

BYZANTIUM (LATER-CONSTANTINOPLE)
(ISTANBUL)

HELLAS   HELLESPONTUS
(GREECE)   TROY   (DARDANELLES)

ACTIUM   PHARSALUS   CAPPADOCIA   MEDIA

ATHENS   ASIA   MINOR   ASSYRIA

SYRIA

ANTIOCH   MESOPOTAMIA

CYPRUS   PALMYRA

CRETE

PHOENICIA

MARE   INTERNUM

(MEDITERRANEAN SEA)   PERSIAN
GULF

ALEXANDRIA

CYRENAICA   ARABIA

AEGYPTUS
(EGYPT)

LIBYA

NILE   RED
SEA

AUGUSTUS AND THE ROMAN EMPIRE

After Caesar's murder, the personal rivalries at Rome finally settled down to two men. One of these was Mark Antony, Caesar's friend and officer. The other was his grandnephew and heir, Octavian. Antony went to live in Alexandria in Egypt, where he married the queen, Cleopatra. Octavian remained in Rome.

When war broke out between Rome and Egypt, the rival fleets met off Actium, in northwestern Greece. Octavian won a decisive victory, and Antony and Cleopatra committed suicide when they went back to Egypt.

The year was 31 B.C., one of the truly important dates in history. Now, for the first time, one man and one man only stood out supreme in the Roman world. This was Octavian, and the Roman Senate and people proclaimed him Emperor. So the Roman Republic came to an end and its place was taken by the Roman Empire. Octavian now changed his name to Augustus, which means "the revered one."

Augustus, as we must now call Rome's first emperor, ruled a long time, from 31 B.C. to 14 A.D. There were universal peace and rejoicing throughout the Empire. The standard of living shot up, trade and business flourished, and people traveled around easily. The birth of Jesus, an event of worldwide significance, occurred during Augustus' reign. Jesus was crucified c. 34, during the rule of Tiberius, the next emperor.

Augustus brought so much happiness and prosperity to the world that his reign came to be known as the Augustan Age. Religion revived. Virgil and other great writers produced their immortal works. Beautiful buildings were built, some of them very large.

Egypt was now part of the Roman Empire. Rome very soon ruled the whole world from Britain to the Euphrates River in Mesopotamia. The whole Mediterranean was hers. In Europe the frontiers of the Empire ran along the Rhine and Danube Rivers; in Africa, along the Sahara Desert; in Asia, along the Euphrates River. Across the Euphrates was the Parthian Empire, the only civilized state that did not belong to Rome. China was too far off to figure in Rome's thinking, though there was some trade between the two.

One of the best things Augustus did was to found schools for the study of law. The excellent laws which the Romans created represent the greatest legislative work of the human race. Augustus' new law schools were especially needed since so much of the world was subject to Rome, and it was important to have the best law possible. Augustus continued Julius Caesar's idea of writing down and classifying the Roman laws. This was such a vast task that it was not finished until the time of the emperor Justinian, who died in 565 A.D.

Roman law recognized the rights of a man to his property. It held that a man could will his goods to whomever he wished; and it insisted that an agreement in writing is binding. It was a humane law and said that a man is innocent until he is proved guilty. Eventually Roman law became the law of Europe and even affected the development of law in England. This happened during the Middle Ages, as we call the centuries between the fall of the Roman Empire and the beginning of the modern age in 1400 A.D.

When we stop to think about all the wars of history, it is hard to believe that Augustus began a period of peace that lasted 250 years. There were a couple of disturbances, to be sure, but no prolonged warfare. And even after the famous Roman Peace was finally destroyed, the Empire itself continued for several centuries. The world has never seen anything like it since.

It was quite natural for people to call Augustus a benefactor of the human race. As emperor, he controlled the armies and foreign policy, and had the power to pass laws. The Senate remained as an advisory body. People still stood for election and became consuls and proconsuls. After all, this great world needed many officials. The provinces, at long last, were justly taxed and governed.

One reason why Augustus wanted the people to keep on electing officials was to make them believe that the good old days of the ancient Roman Republic still continued. He didn't want to appear as a dictator or autocrat, and he actually asked people to call him *Princeps,* or first citizen, instead of Emperor.

44

But actually the elections were a fake, because only Augustus' friends were allowed to run for office. Self-government had ceased, and one-man rule had taken its place. Most people cared very little about this, because they were so glad the civil wars were over.

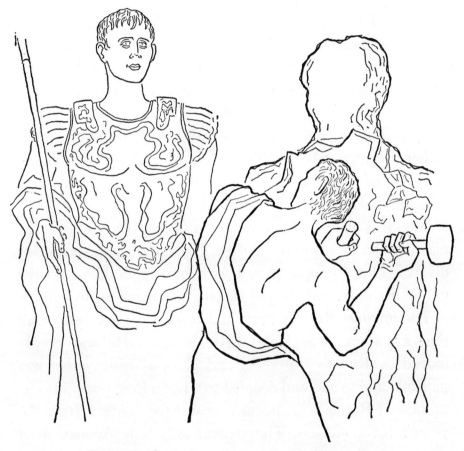

Roman sculptor at work on a statue of Augustus

LITERATURE AND ART
IN THE AUGUSTAN AGE

One thing Augustus tried hard to do was to make people feel happy and have faith in themselves. So he built or repaired eighty-two temples to the gods and urged the Romans to worship the regular gods of the state, such as Jupiter. The days of the old state religion were numbered, however. People found that the Roman gods were pretty cold and did not satisfy the yearnings of the heart. Too often in the past, moreover, religion and politics had been joined together. Besides, other religions were now competing for the attention of men. Among these were Judaism and the new religion, Christianity.

Augustus also tried to strengthen family ties, to make the marriage bond stronger, and to lessen the opportunity for divorce. Other people joined with him in building up the public morality. Artists and writers did their best to help.

The greatest Roman poet, and one of the greatest of all time anywhere, was Virgil (70–19 B.C.). He was deeply moved by Rome's traditions and glorious history. He was patriotic and proud and decided to write a long poem in celebration of Rome. This poem is called the *Aeneid,* from the poem's hero, Aeneas. The *Aeneid* tells how Aeneas, after the destruction of Troy, set out on his long wanderings

46

Aeneas slays King Tournus.
From an episode in Virgil's Aeneid

to Italy. In this way, Virgil tied the beginnings of Rome in with the earliest history of Greece and its war with Troy. He also glorified Augustus, because the family of the emperor, like that of Julius Caesar, traced its descent from Aeneas.

Virgil's story is at once lively and tender. It also has a high moral tone. It shows that Rome's great successes in the past, which won her a world state, were the result of a stern regard for duty. Virgil, more perfectly than any other writer, expressed the ideals of Augustan Rome. He is widely read today.

Another famous poet of the time was Horace (65–8 B.C.). Horace told his reader to forget the civil wars that ended the Roman Republic. Think of the present and enjoy your life, he said, and leave the future to the gods. He recommended good friends, a comfortable house, and fine food as the best things of life. People for hundreds of years have read and enjoyed Horace's *Odes*.

Much of our knowledge of Greek mythology comes from another Augustan poet, Ovid (43 B.C.–17 A.D.). His *Metamorphoses* is a mine of information about the gods and their doings.

Among the writers of prose in the Augustan Age, the greatest was Livy (59 B.C.–17 A.D.). Livy wrote a very moving history of Rome from its beginnings. Some of it is lost, but the parts that remain to us are the most valuable source we have for early Roman history. With Tacitus (55–116 A.D.), the great historian of the Empire, Livy ranks as Rome's finest historian. He admired law and order, and so he glorified the deeds of long ago, hoping to point a moral for the present. Livy's style is grand and dignified. In his work he was accurate and fair, one of the first requirements of a historian!

In the days of Augustus, as in most days, writers and artists needed financial and moral support. The man who helped them more than anyone else was a friend of Augustus, named Maecenas. In a very real sense, the art of the Romans, no less than their literature, owes a great deal to Maecenas. Today we are likely to speak of any patron of the arts as a Maecenas.

Much of the genius of the Romans found expression in fine buildings and beautiful cities. A great deal of the building activity during the Augustan Age went on in the Roman Forum and its neighborhood. The Forum had begun as a simple market place, but by the time of Augustus it was a busy center of the city. Here were the Public Records Office, basilicas (law courts), and the Temple of Concord (Unity). A Sacred Way—used for religious processions and processions of triumphal generals—led through arches down the Forum to the speaker's platform. Even before Augustus the Roman Forum had become so crowded with its buildings and statues that Julius Caesar built his own Forum nearby. Augustus and other emperors followed his example.

Another center of building activity was in the Campus Martius, or Field of Mars, a level stretch of land beside the

The Pantheon

Tiber. One of the most important buildings here was the Pantheon, a temple to all the gods. Its dome illustrates the daring of the Roman engineer, for it was made of solid concrete, 142 feet in diameter, and about as high. The kings and queens of modern Italy are buried in the Pantheon.

Just across the Tiber from the Campus Martius a fine Roman emperor of the second century, Hadrian by name, built his own tomb. Eventually it became famous as the Castel Sant' Angelo, and today it is a landmark of Rome.

Roman architects and engineers built enormous structures, not only temples and public baths and law courts, but also sewers and aqueducts. They took many of their artistic ideas from Greece, but they always adapted them to

50

their own practical use. Nowhere are we more impressed by their genius—and also by the might and wealth of the Roman Empire—than on the Palatine Hill. Here it was that Augustus and later emperors built their enormous palaces.

Roman basilicas were common sights, since the law occupied so large a place in Roman life. The interior was usually divided into a broad central hall, with narrow aisles to the side. There might be a semi-circular wall, or apse, at one end. When the early Christians began to build their churches they did not invent a new style, but copied the common basilicas round about them. Therefore, many a Christian church had an interior consisting simply of a broad hall and side aisles. In others the builders added another hall, or transept, which cut across at a right angle between

Roman Aqueduct

the main hall and the apse. This formed a cross, and it is the pattern of most of the great European cathedrals that were later built.

Probably the most beautiful monument of the Augustan Age was the altar of Peace. It is richly decorated with objects suggesting prosperity, such as flowers and fruit. It shows Augustus and members of his family marching with priests and magistrates to the sacrifices in honor of peace.

The practical Roman preferred realism in his art. We see this in the magnificent portrait sculpture, as well as on the coins and gems. Many successful Roman generals brought shiploads of statues from Greece, and these, too, influenced Roman taste. The Romans loved to decorate arches and columns with carved pictures showing historical events.

Although Rome itself was the center of culture in the Augustan Age, the provinces, too, showed the greatness of the mighty Empire. From one end of the Empire to the other stretched large and beautiful cities. Asia Minor, which today has two cities, boasted 500 in ancient times. All these cities copied Rome and had their own Forums, temples, triumphal arches, and basilicas. Fine paved roads united the cities, and on his arrival the traveler was bound to see familiar aqueducts, bridges, and theaters.

Some of the largest cities were in the East, such as Alexandria in Egypt and Antioch in Syria. Other great cities were built right on the very edges of ancient civilization. Bath, once set among the forests of Britain, was a famous Roman

52

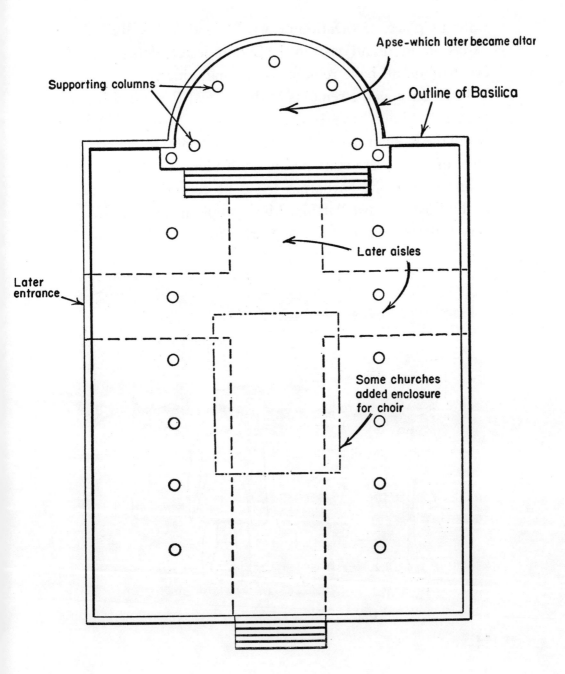

Apse-which later became altar

Outline of Basilica

Supporting columns

Later aisles

Later entrance

Some churches added enclosure for choir

watering place, or vacation resort. Timgad, beside the Sahara desert, Palmyra, an oasis in the Syrian desert, Petra in northern Arabia, all have remains of Roman cities.

Impressive as the remains of these great Roman cities are, even more impressive is the fact that to protect this huge world the Romans needed an army of only 400,000 men. And most of them were stationed way off along the frontiers, on guard against the barbarian tribes of central Europe, and, in the East, against Parthia. Most people in the Empire had very little reason to think of war.

Roman soldier on guard in Africa

AFTER AUGUSTUS

The first rulers who followed Augustus were chosen right from his own family and that of his third wife, Livia. Some of these emperors were good and some bad. One of them, Nero (37–68 A.D.), was a monster.

Nero began his rule well, but he soon turned it into a cruel tyranny with himself as dictator. He murdered his mother and his wife. He filled Rome with spies, who informed on the activities of people. When a terrible fire broke out in Rome the story went round that Nero had started it and that as the city burned, he had played on his lyre and sung songs recalling burning Troy. Nero had nothing to do with the fire, actually. But he had to blame somebody for it, and so he blamed the Christians.

Finally a rebellion broke out against Nero's unjust rule, and he committed suicide.

During the second century A.D. the Romans hit on a different and far better method of choosing an emperor's successor. What the reigning emperor did was to look around him and pick the very ablest man he could find and then adopt him as his son and successor. The result was that during the second century Rome had some of the best rulers any state could enjoy.

Trajan (98–117 A.D.) enlarged the Empire in one important area. The barbarian tribes of central Europe were pressing against the lower Danube, where that great river makes a bend southward. Trajan crossed the river, conquered the district, and made it a province. In those days it was called Dacia, but Roman civilization took such deep root there that ever since it has been called Roumania. As a memorial to his victory Trajan erected a tall column in the Forum which he built at Rome. Today it is a landmark of Rome.

Hadrian (117–138 A.D.), the next emperor, also was concerned with preserving the defenses of the Empire. He discovered that in Britain the Picts of Caledonia—or Scotland, as we call it—were raiding the Roman province. So he built a great wall to keep them out. But the most important thing Hadrian did was to travel all over the Empire. This made his subjects realize that it was the whole Roman world, not just the city of Rome, that was important. Wherever he went Hadrian constructed buildings. Unfortunately, all this cost a good deal, and so did the mere task of running the government. People found it difficult to pay the necessary taxes.

Section of a Roman wall

Roman soldier battling a Pict invader

The reign of Hadrian is often spoken of as the very height of the Roman Empire. A man who lived during Hadrian's time called the whole world a paradise, where men might travel safely by land and sea from one end of the Empire to the other; where, in place of war, cities competed with each other only in their splendor and pleasures. Schools, temples, and gymnasiums greeted one everywhere.

One of the most sensitive of Roman emperors, and one

57

of the finest men who ever lived, was Marcus Aurelius (161–180 A.D.). He was a philosopher and believed in the particular philosophy that appealed to so many Romans. This was Stoicism, which preached a stern regard for duty, the need to be self-reliant, and the brotherhood of man. Marcus Aurelius wrote a book called the *Meditations,* in which he opened his mind and heart. He wrote it in Greek, just as Saint Paul and the Apostles wrote the New Testament in Greek. He wrote it at night by camp fires, for the barbarian tribes were pressing hard, and he had to march to one frontier after another. At the same time, a terrible plague broke out and raged for years. Famine also stalked the Empire.

Clearly, things were not running smoothly. And then the storm broke. In 235 A.D. the Roman peace ended, the barbarians swept from one end of the empire to another, trade stopped, money lost its value, the armies rebelled. During the next half century there were several dozen emperors, some of whom ruled for only a day or two before they were murdered.

What had happened was this. Everything had seemed fine with Augustus. Peace had been established, prosperity was widespread. But people more and more thought just of themselves and of making money, instead of working for the state. In the old days, they had thought of the other fellow and the state. But since a man could not run for office in Augustus' day unless he was the Emperor's friend, public service had come to an end.

That was the big trouble. All hope of self-government had ended. Then the cost of government, as with Hadrian, had grown bigger and bigger. More and more people let the government run their affairs. All, including the soldiers, became discouraged and undisciplined. This made it easier for the barbarian tribes to sweep across the frontier.

Roman general and rebellious soldier

The lesson which the Roman Empire has for us seems to be this: peace and prosperity are not worth the sacrifice of self-government. Once men allow strong rulers to direct their lives, the nation will begin to decay.

The decay of the Roman Empire helps to explain the rapid spread of various religions at this time. Since a happy life on earth was no longer possible for an increasingly large number of people, they began to hope for a happy life at least in the world to come. The third century A.D. was a time of strenuous religious strife. Many religions continued to come out of the East to attract people. One was Mithraism, a sun-worship. But the most important was the religion of Jesus of Nazareth, who had preached love and charity, kindness and joy, the necessity of sacrifice and fellowship.

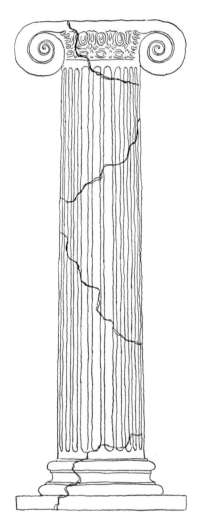

60

CONSTANTINE AND CHRISTIANITY

The barbarian invasions of the Roman Empire during the third century finally came to an end. It was the emperor Diocletian (285–305 A.D.) who finally succeeded in gathering the reins of government firmly in his hands and establishing peace and order. But the world was never the same again. Henceforth the emperors didn't even pretend to rule with the advice of the Senate or anyone else. Mankind now lived under a despotic government.

Nevertheless, Diocletian's successor was one of the most important rulers in history. This was Constantine the Great (306–337 A.D.), who was converted to Christianity and became Rome's first Christian emperor. Once, when marching against his enemies, Constantine had a vision of the Christian cross with the words, "By this sign conquer." He conquered his enemies, and after his victory he turned to the religion of the Christians. Now the Christians, instead of being persecuted as they had been for so long, saw their religion become the state religion.

Constantine helped to build Christian churches and helped the bishops to convert heretics into true believers. In 325 he summoned the first world-wide council of the church. It was held at Nicaea in Asia Minor, and matters of what Christians were to believe were decided on. Today most

Christians recite the Nicene Creed—a statement of what they believe. This creed is almost the same as the one settled upon at Nicaea.

Constantine also founded a new capital of the Roman Empire. He named it after himself, Constantine's City, or Constantinople. Today it is called Istanbul. Its location on the Bosporus, leading up to the Black Sea, is superbly beautiful. But the cost of the new capital and its decoration—to say nothing of the cost of the army and the many officials—was tremendous. In order to meet it Constantine taxed the people heavily. Many farmers, unable to pay the tax, fled to the cities where they would not be noticed so easily by the tax collectors.

With more and more farmers deserting their land, the Roman Empire was threatened with famine. For that reason Constantine decreed that farmers must remain on their land. This was the beginning of the serfdom of the next centuries, whereby people were bound to the soil and subject to the will of the man who owned it.

Roman farmer plowing with oxen

Mongol invaders

Constantine had wanted a new capital because he was eager to get out of Rome with all its reminders of a more democratic past. He thought, too, that as a dictator he should have his own imperial capital. He placed it in the East because that was closest to the lower Danube and Euphrates Rivers, where the chief danger of barbarian invasion seemed to lie.

In the years ahead the barbarians kept pressing on the frontiers and occasionally got across and raided the Empire.

63

Alaric and the Goths, the Vandals, and Attila the Hun from northern Europe were some of the worst invaders. In order to cope with these dangers, the Roman Empire was divided into Western and Eastern halves. In 476 A.D. the Western Roman Empire went down completely before the barbarians. German chieftains sat on the throne of Augustus. Europe was broken up into different kingdoms and entered a new phase of history, that of the Middle Ages. The Bishop of Rome, known as the Pope, did what he could to protect the people of the West from harsh barbarian rule.

The Eastern Roman Empire, however, with its capital at Constantinople, survived the onslaught of the barbarians. In fact, it stood till 1453 A.D. when the Mohammedan Turks finally overwhelmed this last stronghold of the ancient world.

German chieftain on the throne of Augustus

ROME'S LEGACY

Fortunately for the future, the German tribesmen who became the new rulers in the West had been converted by missionaries to Christianity before they entered the Empire. They were also eager to learn the ways of civilization. Thus much of the ancient civilization was able to survive.

This civilization was Roman. But, as we have seen, the Romans borrowed much from ancient Greece, and the Christian religion came from the Jews. So the civilization that survived was a combination of Roman, Greek, and Semitic.

The most important single thing to survive was the Christian religion. Next we must place the Roman idea of law. The Roman genius in governing and running a huge state successfully for centuries must also rank high on our list. Then, too, there is much to be learned from Roman art, literature, and philosophy. The Latin language itself survived and has remained the language of the Catholic Church. Through the centuries Latin developed in different lands into such modern languages as Italian, Portuguese, and French. Much of the English language has also developed from the Latin.

The civilization of ancient times—Roman, Greek, and Semitic—is the basis of our own civilization. The ancient world was never perfect, but it did reach great heights. We

65

can profit by the mistakes made by those men of long ago and we can learn from their experience.

Consider the different foods enjoyed in different parts of the Roman Empire, the different clothing worn, the many gods and forms of worship. Consider not only the different races and languages but also the fact that some people were rough mountaineers and others were highly civilized city dwellers. To an extraordinary degree racial hatred and discrimination were missing. And then consider the peace that lasted for 250 years. It ended largely because the Romans gave up self-government. Rome's challenge seems to be to keep and improve the democracy we have and to get the peace which she herself once had.

A FEW OF THE WORDS WE HAVE INHERITED FROM THE ROMANS

ADJECTIVE. A word used with a noun to denote the quality of the thing named. From the Latin *adjectivus,* that which is added.

AGRICULTURE. The science of cultivating the ground and raising crops. From the Latin *ager,* field, plus *cultura,* cultivation.

ALUMNUS. A graduate of a university or college. From the Latin *alere,* to nourish.

AMBIGUOUS. Doubtful, uncertain. From the Latin *ambigere,* to go about uncertainly, to wander.

BISECT. To divide into two parts. From the Latin *bi-,* two, plus *secare, sectum,* to cut.

CAMPUS. The grounds surrounding a college or university. In Latin, a field.

CEMENT. A mixture used in a soft state to join bricks and stones, which dries as hard as a rock. From the Latin *caementum,* a rough, unhewn stone.

CONSENT. To agree, or to yield to pressure or necessity. From the Latin *consentire,* to feel together.

GENIUS. A person of more than ordinary intelligence or ability. In Roman religion, a guardian spirit.

IMPETUS. Power derived from motion. From the Latin *in* plus *petere,* to rush upon, to attack by force.

INCENSE. The fragrance or smoke given off by burning herbs or gums. Also, to annoy or irritate. From the Latin *incendere,* to burn.

INCH. The twelfth part of a foot. From the Latin *uncia,* the twelfth part of anything.

JANITOR. A person who is in charge of a building. From Janus, the Roman god who had charge of the gates of heaven.

LIBRARIAN. One who has charge of a library. From the Latin *liber,* a book.

LINIMENT. A preparation, thinner than an ointment, to be rubbed on the skin. From the Latin *linimentum,* that which is spread or smeared.

MINISTER. One who renders service, as the minister of a church, a prime minister, &c. In Latin, a servant, an attendant.

MISER. A person who lives miserably in order to hoard money or the like. In Latin, a miserable person.

PAUPER. A poor person in both English and Latin.

PERCOLATOR. A form of coffee pot in which heated water filters through the coffee grounds. From the Latin *percolare,* to filter through.

PREMIUM. Commonly used in America to mean something given away with purchased merchandise. From the Latin *praemium,* profit, reward.

SERPENT. A snake. From the Latin *serpere,* to creep.

SUCCEED. To be successful. From the Latin *succedere,* to go from under, to ascend.

TORRID. Hot and dry. From the Latin *torrere,* to dry, bake, roast.

VACUUM. A space entirely devoid of matter. In Latin, an empty space.

INDEX

68